Helping Children See Jesus

ISBN: 978-1-64104-044-0

THE LORDSHIP OF CHRIST
New Testament Volume 7
Life of Christ Part 7

Author: Ruth B. Greiner
Illustrator: Frances H. Hertzler
Colorization courtesy of Good Life Ministries
Typesetting and Layout: Morgan Melton, Patricia Pope

© 2018 Bible Visuals International
PO Box 153, Akron, PA 17501-0153
Phone: (717) 859-1131
www.biblevisuals.org

All rights reserved. No part of this publication may be reproduced, stored in a retrieval system or transmitted in any form by any means, electronic, mechanical, photocopy, recording or otherwise, without the prior permission of the publisher, except as provided by USA copyright law.

RELATED ITEMS

To access related items (such as activities, memory verse posters and translated texts) please visit our web store at www.biblevisuals.org and enter 1007 at the top right of the web page. You may need to reduce the zoom setting to get the search box.

FREE TEXT DOWNLOAD

To obtain a FREE printable copy of the English teaching text (PDF format) under Product Format, please scroll down and select Extra–PDF Teacher Text Download. Then under Language select English before clicking the ADD TO CART button to place in your shopping cart. Other languages are available at an additional cost from the Language menu. When checking out, use coupon code XTACSV17 at checkout and click on Apply Coupon to receive the discount on the English text.

That at the name of Jesus every knee should bow . . . and . . . every tongue should confess that Jesus Christ is Lord, to the glory of God the Father. Philippians 2:10a, 11

© Bible Visuals International Inc

Lesson 1
FEEDING FIVE THOUSAND—AND MORE!

NOTE TO THE TEACHER

At the time He fed the 5,000 men, apparently about one-half of the public ministry of our Lord Jesus Christ was past. Yet the Bible records only one instance in that year-and-a-half that the disciples used the name "Lord" when speaking about or to the Lord Jesus. (See Matthew 8:25. That same event is recorded in Mark 4:36-41 and Luke 8:22-25. In those passages the word "Master" is used rather than "Lord.") It is not entirely clear whether or not it was the disciples who used the name "Lord" in Matthew 13:51.

Others who spoke to the Lord Jesus did call Him Lord. In all probability they used the name simply as a title of respect. They recognized Him as a master. However, the name "Lord" when spoken of the Lord Jesus Christ, actually means *Jehovah* (a name for God). He is "Emmanuel," *God with us*.

In the first lesson in this series, the name "Lord" is not used in the Scriptures. In the second lesson, it is used three times. First, Peter calls, "Lord, if it be You. . ." Then he cries, "Lord, save me!" Later his confession that Christ is the Son of the living God, begins, "Lord, to whom shall we go?"

After the transfiguration (the third lesson in this series), the disciples use the term "Lord" with growing frequency. They had begun to understand that He, Jesus Christ, is indeed the Lord.

Let it never be forgotten, whether or not He is so recognized, He is always the Lord (God the Son). Because He is Lord, He has the right to be Master.

Scripture to be studied: Matthew 14:21-31; Mark 6:30-44; Luke 9:10-17; John 6:1-15, 51-66

The *aim* of the lesson: To help your students understand that the Lord Jesus Christ, the Creator of all things, is able to meet every need–spiritual and physical.

What your students should *know*: The young boy obediently gave all his lunch to Jesus.

What your students should *feel*: A desire to be obedient.

What your students should *do*:

Unsaved: Believe in the Lord Jesus Christ.

Saved: Give themselves entirely to the Lord.

Lesson outline (for the teacher's and students' notebooks):

1. Jesus takes the disciples apart to rest (Luke 9:10; Mark 6:30-31).
2. Jesus teaches the crowds that follow Him (Matthew 14:13-14; Mark 6:32-34; Luke 9:11; John 6:1-3).
3. Jesus feeds the multitude with five buns and two fish (Matthew 14:15-19; Mark 6:35-41; Luke 9:12-16; John 6:4-11).
4. Jesus is the Living Bread who gives everlasting life (Matthew 14:19-21; Mark 6:41-44; Luke 9:16-17; John 6:11-15, 51-66).

The verses to be memorized:

That at the name of Jesus every knee should bow . . . and . . . every tongue should confess that Jesus Christ is Lord, to the glory of God the Father. (Philippians 2:10a, 11)

THE LESSON

The Lord Jesus is known by many names. Among them are: Son of Man; the Saviour; the Lamb of God; the Lord; Jesus Christ. Each name has meaning. "Jesus" for example, means *One who saves from sin*. (See Matthew 1:21.) "Christ" means *the promised One [Messiah]*. (See John 1:11; 4:25; 17:3; Luke 24:46.)

In this series we are going to learn the meaning of His name "Lord." So, in your notebook, at the top of the page, write THE LORDSHIP OF CHRIST. Under that, write the memory verses (Philippians 2:10a, 11). Now write:

The "Lord" means *Jehovah* (a name for God).

The Lord Jesus is *God with us*. (See Matthew 1:23.)

Because Jesus is Lord, He has the right to be Master.

As we study the lessons in this series, we shall learn that God the Son, the Lord Jesus Christ, is worthy of our obedience, our gifts, our worship, our service.

For hundreds and hundreds of years people had been waiting for the coming of the Son of God to earth. (See, for example, the promise of His coming in Isaiah 9:6.) Those who studied the Word of God, knew that the One who would come would be a Prophet. (See Deuteronomy 18:15, 18-19.) They knew, also, that He would be a King. (See Jeremiah 23:5; Zechariah 9:9.) Now One had come who did many miracles. Closely the people watched Him, the Lord Jesus Christ. And they listened to His teaching.

1. JESUS TAKES THE DISCIPLES APART TO REST
Luke 9:10; Mark 6:30-31

One day the 12 disciples had returned from a very busy, tiring preaching trip. (See Matthew 10:5-8; Luke 9:1-2.) They wanted to tell Jesus all that had happened. But there were so many people–hundreds, perhaps thousands!–thronging around Jesus, that His disciples had no time even to eat or rest.

Show Illustration #1

Jesus knew what the disciples needed. So He said to them, "Come along to a quiet place where you can rest awhile."

So Jesus and the twelve disciples got into a boat and started across the Sea (Lake) of Galilee, headed for a quiet place near Bethsaida (of Julias).

2. JESUS TEACHES THE CROWDS THAT FOLLOW HIM
Matthew 14:13-14; Mark 6:32-34; Luke 9:11; John 6:1-3

Many people, however, had seen them leave. The news had quickly spread to nearby towns: "Jesus is crossing the lake!" Men and women and boys and girls had seen His power in healing sick people. They wanted to be with Him so they could hear and see more.

Great crowds hurried on foot around the shore of Lake Galilee. And there they were–waiting!–when Jesus and His disciples arrived. Was He angry that they had followed Him? No! He felt sorry for them. They needed someone to lead them and care for them. So Jesus welcomed the people.

But how do you suppose the disciples felt? They could not talk alone to Jesus as they had planned. They could not rest with those crowds around them. And how could they eat?

The people gathered on the hillside near the lake. Then Jesus began to teach them. More and more people came–hundreds of them–men, women and children. Soon there were 1,000, then 2,000, 3,000 thousand. In all there were 5,000 men–besides women and children! They listened as Jesus taught them. Some of the people who had come were sick. Perhaps they came for this very reason, having heard that He healed sick people. And do you know what? Jesus healed them that very day!

All afternoon the people listened. They seemed to forget that it was time to eat. They had never heard anyone as wonderful as Jesus.

Show Illustration #2

Then evening came. The disciples had waited as long as they could. Finally they said to Jesus. "It is very late and this is a lonely place. Send the people to the nearby villages to find food and places to stay for the night."

But Jesus said, "They do not have to go away. You give them something to eat."

Philip (one of the disciples) exclaimed, "Two hundred days' wages would not buy enough bread for all of these people to have even a little to eat!"

Jesus asked the disciples, "How much bread is here? Go and see."

3. JESUS FEEDS THE MULTITUDE WITH FIVE BUNS AND TWO FISH
Matthew 14:15-19; Mark 6:35-41; Luke 9:12-16; John 6:4-11

The disciples went among the people, looking for food. Returning to Jesus, Andrew alone had good news. But even as he told Jesus about it, he did not seem happy. "There is a boy here who has five buns and two little fish. But what good is that among so many people?"

"Bring them to Me," Jesus said.

Show Illustration #3

What will Jesus do with my five buns and two fish? that hungry boy wondered. He listened carefully as Christ Jesus instructed the disciples to have the people sit down on the green grass in groups of 50 and 100, He watched closely as Jesus took his lunch, and, looking up to Heaven, thanked God for the buns and the fish. (And, certainly, He thanked His Father for the boy who had given his lunch!)

4. JESUS IS THE LIVING BREAD WHO GIVES EVERLASTING LIFE
Matthew 14:19-21; Mark 6:41-44; Luke 9:16-17; John 6:11-15, 51-66

Show Illustration #4

Then Jesus started breaking the buns and dividing the fish. He gave some to Philip and to Andrew and to each of the other disciples. In turn, the disciples gave food to each person. They returned to Jesus to get more. Back and forth they went until everyone had enough–and more than enough!–to eat.

Then Jesus told the disciples to gather the food that the people had not eaten, so nothing would be wasted. They put it into baskets–1, 2, 3, 4, 5–12 baskets were filled with leftover bread and fish! Think of it: there were twelve baskets left from the lunch of one boy–a boy who had obediently given everything he had to Jesus.

When the people saw the miracle Jesus had done, they exclaimed, "He is the Prophet whom we have been expecting!" Some doubtless remembered the promise that the One who was to come would satisfy the poor with bread. (See Psalm 132:15.)

The crowd was so enthusiastic that they decided to take Jesus by force and make Him King. Knowing this, Jesus immediately left the people and went up into a mountain alone. Long, long afterwards a day would come when He would be King. But before this could happen, He would have to die. He explained this to them the next day, saying, "I am the living bread which came down from Heaven. If any man eat of this bread, he will live forever. And the bread that I shall give is My flesh, which I shall give for the life of the world."

That He would give His flesh (meaning He would *die,*) disappointed those who expected to make Him their King. They wanted a living King, not a dead one. And, from that time, many who had followed Him turned back. They did not recognize Him as the Lord Jesus Christ, God the Son. So they refused to follow Him.

What about the disciples? Did they realize that Jesus Christ is the Lord? Apparently not at that moment. For we are told they lacked understanding. (See Mark 6:52.)

That He could heal the sick, they knew. That He could feed multitudes, they knew. Apparently they did not yet understand that the Miracle-worker was the Creator. (See John 1:3.) The Creator is the Lord–the Lord Jesus Christ.

What about you? Have you believed in Him, the Lord and Saviour Jesus Christ? "He that believeth on Me," He said, "hath everlasting life" (John 6:48).

If you are already a believer in Christ, will you, like the boy, give everything to Him? How can you do less? He is the Lord!

Lesson 2
WALKING ON THE WATER

NOTE TO THE TEACHER

In the past we have had a number of lessons on the miracles performed by the Lord Jesus Christ. We have another before us. Because Satan is a great imitator, it is possible for him to do certain things which could be considered miraculous. We should always be able to recognize the hand of God in genuine miracles. Maybe it will help you and your students to remember these four facts regarding Bible miracles:

1. Each miracle met a human need in a superhuman way.
2. Each miracle overruled the usual forces of nature.
3. Each miracle revealed something of the power and glory of God.
4. Each miracle taught a lesson.

It should be observed that when the Lord Jesus did miracles on earth, He was acting according to His divine character. As Creator together with God the Father, He made the heavens, the earth, and everything in them. He made grain, which (in the course of time) would be made into bread. But it was equally easy for Him to make the bread im-mediately and feed 5,000 men, besides women and children! He had created grapes. But He could as easily make wine instantaneously.

He gave life. He gave health. He gathered the waters together in the third day of creation and called them "seas." He set a bound on the seas so that they could not cover the earth. (See Psalm 104:6-9.) And, as God the Son on earth, He controlled the waters, as we shall see in this lesson.

The Lord, Jesus Christ can protect His people *in* the storms. Or, if He chooses, He can stop the storms. He is Master over every situation. A person need not be afraid of anything if he knows the Lord Jesus Christ. Help your pupils to understand this.

Scripture to be studied: Matthew 14:22-34; Mark 6:45-56; John 6:15-21, 28-29, 47, 64, 67-69

The *aim* of the lesson: To teach that Jesus is the Master of every situation.

What your students should *feel*: A real purpose of heart to obey the Lord absolutely.

What your students should *know*: Because Jesus Christ is the Lord, His children owe Him complete obedience.

What your students should *do*:
Unsaved: Believe that Jesus Christ is the Son of God.
Saved: Let Jesus Christ be the Master of every situation.

Lesson outline (for the teacher's and students' notebooks):

1. The disciples cross Lake Galilee (Matthew 14:22-23; Mark 6:45-46; John 6:15-16).
2. A storm threatens the disciples (Matthew 14:24; Mark 6:47-48; John 6:17-19).
3. Jesus walking on the water, comes to the disciples (Matthew 14:25-27; Mark 6:48-50; John 6:19-20).
4. The disciples recognize that Jesus is the Son of God (Matthew 14: 28-34; Mark 6:51-56; John 6:21, 28-29, 47, 64, 67-69).

The verses to be memorized:

That at the name of Jesus every knee should bow . . . and . . . every tongue should confess that Jesus Christ is Lord, to the glory of God the Father. (Philippians 2:10a, 11)

THE LESSON

Have you ever been afraid? of the dark? of a storm? of a strange person? or an animal? I am sure you have. We all know what it means to be afraid. One day even the disciples of the Lord Jesus became afraid. Are you listening?

1. THE DISCIPLES CROSS LAKE GALILEE
Matthew 14:22-23; Mark 6:45-46; John 6:15-16

Show Illustration #5

When the disciples left Bethsaida (Julias) in their boat, the water was calm and the sky was clear. They had been on Lake Galilee many times. Sometimes Jesus went with them. Other times He did not. This time He had remained alone on the mountain. Jesus had instructed the disciples to sail across the lake toward Bethsaida (of Galilee) on the way to Capernaum.

As they sailed away, leaving the Lord Jesus to pray alone, the disciples had much to think and talk about. Earlier that very day they had hoped to find a place where they could be alone with Jesus. But the people in the surrounding villages had hurried along the shore to be with Jesus. Five thousand men plus women and children had crowded around Jesus to hear Him speak. They had stayed and stayed! Oh, it had seemed like such a long day!

At last the disciples had told Jesus to send the people away to get something to eat. But Jesus had not done that. Instead, He had performed a miracle. He had taken the little lunch of one boy, multiplied it, and fed those thousands of hungry people. No one else could have done such a mighty act. But the Lord Jesus is different from everyone else. He is the Lord– God the Son!

Surely the disciples were glad to have this same Jesus as their Friend. They had seen Him do many wonderful miracles. Once He had changed water into wine. He had made sick people well. He even had raised the dead to life! The Lord Jesus could do all things. By now His disciples should have understood that they could trust him for every need in their lives. Since He could feed thousands of people with a boy's lunch, He could certainly care for 12 disciples!

2. A STORM THREATENS THE DISCIPLES
Matthew 14:24; Mark 6:47-48; John 6:17-19

But now they were in a boat. And Jesus was not with them. They must hurry across the bay to Bethsaida where they hoped Jesus would join them and go with them across the lake to Capernaum.

Show Illustration #6

The disciples held on to the sails. The lake, which had been calm and peaceful,

– 21 –

had grown rough. A strong wind blew and big waves rocked the boat. The men pulled hard on the oars but the wind and the waves pushed the boat off their course. The waves grew bigger. They splashed into the boat as the storm grew worse.

The sky had grown dark and the disciples felt strangely alone as their boat tossed back and forth on the rough water. Finally they were in the middle of the lake. No matter how hard they tried, they could not row the boat to Bethsaida. The disciples must have been worried about their safety. If only Jesus had come with them! But it had been a busy day amid He had wanted to be alone with His heavenly Father.

They rowed and rowed–one hour, two hours, three. On and on they struggled against the wind and the waves.

3. JESUS WALKING ON THE WATER, COMES TO THE DISCIPLES
Matthew 14:25-27; Mark 6:48-50; John 6:19-20

Show Illustration #7

Much later (sometime between three and six o'clock in the morning) the disciples saw something strange. They all saw it–Peter, James, John, Philip and the others. Something or someone was coming towards them–and that someone was walking right on top of the waves! The disciples cried, "It is a ghost!"

A voice responded, "It is I. Do not be afraid!"

The disciples had heard this voice before. There was only One who spoke like that. It was the voice of the Lord Jesus Christ. And He was walking right on top of the waves (just as you and I would walk on dry ground)! Deep water, stormy winds, high waves, the darkness of night–none of these could keep Jesusfrom being with His disciples when they needed Him. The disciples had never before seen Jesus do this kind of miracle.

4. THE DISCIPLES RECOGNIZE THAT JESUS IS THE SON OF GOD
Matthew 14:28-34; Mark 6:51-56; John 6:21, 28-29, 47, 64, 67-69

Peter called to Him, "Lord, if it is really You, tell me to come to You on the water."

"Come," the Lord called.

Peter stepped over the side of the boat. He saw the dark water and felt it under his feet. He started to walk toward Jesus. He, Peter, was walking on the water! But then he looked away from Jesus. He saw the storm. He saw the high waves. Suddenly he became frightened. He looked down at the heaving water.

Then he began to sink. Something was wrong! "Lord, save me!" he cried.

Show Illustration #8

Immediately the Lord Jesus reached out His hand and caught hold of Peter. "What little faith you have," Jesus said. "Why did you doubt?"

The words of the Lord Jesus must have made Peter ashamed of himself. Instead of keeping his eyes on Jesus and trusting Him, he looked at the storm and became afraid.

As Jesus and Peter together stepped into the boat the wind and the storm suddenly stopped. The disciples were glad. Jesus was with them and they were safe! Immediately they worshiped Him, saying, "It is true. You really are the Son of God!" At last they began to realize that the Miracle-worker, Jesus, is indeed God the Son.

Later that day, the crowds whom Jesus had fed the day before, followed Him to Capernaum. One of the questions they asked Him was, "What shall we do, that we might work the works of God" (John 6:28)?

Jesus answered, "This is the work of God, that you believe on Him whom God hath sent."

Whom had God sent? The Lord Jesus Christ.

He added, "He that believeth on Me hath everlasting life." Then, He who sees each heart, said sadly, "You have seen Me, and believe not" (John 6:36).

Moments later, many of the people went back. Only the day before, they wanted Him to be their King. Now they refused to follow Him. Turning to His disciples Jesus said, "Will you also go away?"

Peter asked, "Lord, to whom shall we go? You have the words of eternal life. And we believe and are sure that You are the Christ, the Son of the living God."

Good for Peter! Three times, within only a few hours, he called Jesus "Lord." Once when He saw Jesus walking on the water: "Lord, if it is You . . ." Again when he was sinking in the stormy sea: "Lord, save me!" And the third time, "Lord, to whom shall we go?" Now he understands that the Lord Jesus Christ is "the Son of the living God"–and as such is God Himself.

As the Lord Jesus was concerned about Peter and the disciples, so He is concerned about you. (See Hebrews 13:8.) What He wants most for you to have is His life–everlasting life. He came to earth to die, that you might go to Heaven to live.

You are hearing this lesson today because God wants you to know that the Lord Jesus Christ is His Son. Have you believed this? Have you confessed with your mouth that Jesus Christ is the Lord?

Because Jesus Christ is Lord, He is entitled to your complete obedience, if you are His child. If you purpose in your heart *always to obey Him absolutely,* you may be certain of this: *He will always guide you perfectly.*

Lesson 3
THE TRANSFIGURATION

NOTE TO THE TEACHER

In the last two lessons you have taught that: (1) those who trust in Jesus Christ as Lord and Saviour can be certain that *He will meet every need in His own way;* (2) *the Lord Jesus Christ controls the elements of nature.* In this lesson we see *a picture of the Lord Jesus Christ as glorious Lord of the future.* The day is coming when He will be crowned King of kings and Lord of lords. Then every knee will bow to Him as Lord and every tongue will confess that Jesus Christ is Lord, to the glory of God the Father.

The purpose of this lesson is to help your pupils to see that, at His transfiguration, He revealed His future glory. Because He is the Lord of glory, we should utterly obey Him.

Scripture to be studied: Matthew 16:13-17:13; Mark 8:27-9:13; Luke 9:18-36; 2 Peter 1:16-19

The *aim* of the lesson: To help your students to see that, at His transfiguration, the Lord Jesus revealed His future glory.

What your students should *know*: Because Jesus Christ is the Lord of glory, we should obey Him unreservedly.

What your students should *feel*: A real desire to have the Lord Jesus control their lives.

What your students should *do*: Yield their lives to the Lord Jesus and willingly obey Him.

Lesson outline (for the teacher's and students' notebooks):

1. Jesus tells His disciples He must suffer (Matthew 16:13-28; Mark 8:27-9:1; Luke 9:18-27).
2. Jesus prays to His Father (Matthew 17:1; Mark 9:2; Luke 9:28).
3. The shining brightness (glory) of God shines through Jesus (Matthew 17:2-4; Mark 9:3-6; Luke 9:29-33).
4. God commands the disciples to listen to His Son (Matthew 17:5-13; Mark 9:7-13; Luke 9:34-36).

The verses to be memorized:

That at the name of Jesus every knee should bow . . .and . . . every tongue should confess that Jesus Christ is Lord, to the glory of God the Father. (Philippians 2:10a, 11)

THE LESSON

Have you ever tried to walk on top of the water? Could you do it? No! It is impossible. Do you think you could stop the wind from blowing? No! No matter what you said or did, you could not stop the wind.

Yet Peter, James, John, and the other disciples had seen Jesus do these very things. They had seen Him walk on the water of Lake Galilee. They had also seen Him stop the stormy wind from blowing.

1. JESUS TELLS HIS DISCIPLES HE MUST SUFFER
Matthew 16:13-28; Mark 8:27-9:1; Luke 9:18-27

Later the Lord Jesus asked His disciples, "Tell Me, who do people say that I am?"

They answered, "Some say that You are John the Baptist; others, Elijah. Others say You are Jeremiah or some other prophet."

Show Illustration #9

Then Jesus asked a most important question, "Who do *you* say that I am?"

John was silent. James was silent. Philip and Andrew said not a word. Only one disciple gave an answer. He was the same one who had tried to walk on the water to meet Jesus on Lake Galilee only a short time before. What is his name? *(Peter.)*

What did Peter think of Jesus? Listen to his answer: "You are the Christ of God, the Son of the living God." Peter knew that Jesus, even though He looked like other men, was more than a man. He is the Lord Jesus Christ, the promised One, the Saviour Son of God. He is the One who can meet every need, whether it is hunger, or sickness, or death. He is the Lord of the stormy sea, the Lord of the wind.

It was after Peter gave this testimony that the Lord Jesus taught the disciples something they did not want to believe: that He must suffer many things; He would be rejected; He would be killed. He also taught them that after three days He would rise again. The disciples did not want Jesus to die. They wanted Him to become their King on earth now. But no! Jesus taught them that He must suffer. So they were troubled.

Peter took Jesus aside and said, "Lord, this will never happen to You." Now this was the wrong thing for Peter to say. He had said the right thing earlier when he confessed Jesus was "the Christ, the Son of the living God." But now Peter was wrong and Jesus rebuked him. Christ Jesus knows all things. He knew that He had come to earth for the very purpose of dying.

2. JESUS PRAYS TO HIS FATHER
Matthew 17:1; Mark 9:2; Luke 9:28

Show Illustration #10

A few days later Jesus went up into a high mountain (probably Mount Hermon). He took only three of His disciples with Him–Peter, James and John.

As they climbed the mountain with Jesus, the three must have wondered, *Why is He taking us up here?* They knew that often He went alone to the quietness of a mountain to pray. But why was He taking them with Him? Up they went–away from the people and away from the other disciples. At last they reached the place that the Lord Jesus had chosen. Then Jesus began to pray. Peter, James and John should have prayed, too. Perhaps they did for a little while. But they were tired and fell asleep. Jesus may have been tired also. But that did not keep him from praying. He prayed, not because He *had* to but because He *wanted* to. He, the Son of God, had no sin to confess. But He prayed because He loved His heavenly Father and wanted to talk with Him. He often spoke to His Father about the people on earth–the ones who had believed on Him. He prayed too for those who turned away from Him and refused to believe in Him.

– 23 –

3. THE SHINING BRIGHTNESS (GLORY) OF GOD SHINES THROUGH JESUS
Matthew 17:2-4; Mark 9:3-6; Luke 9:29-33

We do not know how long He prayed there on the mountain. But suddenly something very strange happened. As the Lord Jesus prayed, a change came over Him. His face shone like the sun. His clothing became shining–as bright as the light, as white as the snow on the mountaintop. Nobody in the world could make clothes so white and shining. (In those days kings and priests wore the whitest clothes they could find to show their high office. But here the clothes of Jesus were brighter and whiter than the whitest clothes any king had ever worn.) This brightness did not come upon Jesus from the outside. It came from within. Why? Because Jesus is God the Son and the glory of God was in Him. It was the glory which He had with the Father even before the world was. (See John 17:5.)

Show Illustration #11

Blinking their sleepy eyes in the dazzling brightness, the three disciples saw that two others had joined the Lord Jesus: Moses (who had died almost 1,500 years before!) and Elijah (who had lived on earth about 900 years before!). Moses had been used by God to give the Law to His people. Then after serving God for many years, Moses had died. Elijah had been a great prophet of God who had warned the people of God (and their king) to repent. When his work on earth was done, Elijah was taken to Heaven without dying. Now, after so many hundreds of years, these two appeared in heavenly splendor on the mountain with Jesus–and the three were talking together! In those glorious moments they talked about the things that were to happen to Jesus–how He soon would accomplish the plan of God by going to Jerusalem to die. (See Luke 9:31.)

When it seemed as if Moses and Elijah were going to leave, Peter wanted them to stay. He was so terrified by what he had seen that he did not know what to say. Instead of remaining silent as he should have done, Peter said, "Lord, it is good that we are here. Let us make three tents–one for Thee, one for Moses, and one for Elijah."

4. GOD COMMANDS THE DISCIPLES TO LISTEN TO HIS SON
Matthew 17:5-13; Mark 9:7-13; Luke 9:34-36

As Peter said this, a shining cloud appeared. It was not a watery cloud but a heavenly cloud of glory. From that shining cloud came a voice–the voice of God–saying, "This is My own dear Son, the Beloved One, with whom I am well pleased. Listen to Him!" Quiet, Peter! Listen to My Son!

Show Illustration #12

When they heard the voice of God the Father, the three disciples were so frightened they fell on their faces to the ground. But Jesus touched them, saying, "Stand up. Do not be afraid."

Peter, James, and John lifted their heads. They looked around. Moses and Elijah were gone! They saw Jesus alone–no longer in His shining glory but again in His perfect humanity. Moses and Elijah had been men just like the disciples. But Jesus is the Lord. He is the Son of God. He is the One to be obeyed. The voice of God said, "Listen to Him."

The three disciples had seen something they would never forget. They had seen the glory of Jesus, the Lord. From this time on they should have known that it was right that He should suffer and die as He had said He would, for that is what God had planned. Then some day (which is still future) Jesus Christ will rule in all His glory as King of all kings and Lord of lords. In that day every knee will bow before Him and every tongue will confess that Jesus Christ is Lord, to the glory of God the Father.

As they came down the mountain, Jesus commanded the three disciples not to tell anyone about the things they had seen and heard on the mountain until after He had risen from the dead. What a secret!

Those three had much to think about and to talk to each other about. But, strange as it may seem, they could not seem to understand what Jesus had meant when He spoke of rising from the dead. They continually talked about it among themselves. However, they simply could not realize that Jesus would have to suffer and die before receiving the glory which they had seen when He was transfigured before them.

Why the Lord Jesus told the three not to tell what they had seen, we do not know. It *may* be that our Lord knew that, even if they were to tell others about His transfiguration, they would not be believed until after the greater miracle of His resurrection. Or *perhaps* their telling of such an experience at this time might have resulted in physical danger, even death, to Peter, James, and John. We do not *know* why the Lord Jesus commanded that they not tell. But He is to be obeyed. He is the Lord!

Years later, when the disciples perfectly understood the death and resurrection of our Lord, they told their secret. John wrote: "And we beheld His glory, the glory as of the only Begotten of the Father" (John 1:14). And Peter explained that they "were eyewitnesses of His majesty. For He received from God the Father honor and glory, when there came such a voice to Him from the excellent glory, 'This is My beloved Son, in whom I am well pleased.' And this voice which came from Heaven we heard, when we were with Him on the holy mount" (2 Peter 1:16-18).

If you have believed in the Son of God and received Him as Saviour, He lives in your heart. Your greatest desire should be to have Him control your life. As Lord, He is entitled to your perfect obedience. Instead of wanting your own way, you should yield to Him, willingly obeying your Lord. He will never force you to obey Him. But if you bow to Him completely, you will have His perfect guidance always. (See Psalm 32:8.) "I beseech you . . . by the mercies of God, that ye present your bodies a living sacrifice, holy, acceptable unto God, which is your reasonable service. And be not conformed to this world: but be ye transformed by the renewing of your mind, that ye may prove what is that good, and acceptable, and perfect, will of God" (Romans 12:1-2).

Lesson 4
THE LORDSHIP OF CHRIST

Scripture to be studied: Acts 2:36; Acts 10:36; Mark 16:15, 20; Colossians 3:24

The *aim* of the lesson: To prove that Jesus Christ is Master, Ruler, Lord.

What your students should *know*: One day everyone will bow before Jesus and confess that He is Lord.

What your students should *feel*: A willingness to let Jesus be Saviour and Lord.

What your students should *do*:
Unsaved: Let Christ be their Saviour today.
Saved: Let Christ rule their lives.

Lesson outline (for the teacher's and students' notebooks):
1. Jesus wants us to give ourselves to Him (Romans 12:1).
2. Jesus is the eternal Son of God, Creator of all (Hebrews 1:1-2).
3. Jesus proved He is Lord by the miracles He did (Hebrews 2:4).
4. Jesus proved His power over sin and death (Hebrews 1:3).

The verses to be memorized:

That at the name of Jesus every knee should bow . . . and . . . every tongue should confess that Jesus Christ is Lord, to the glory of God the Father. (Philippians 2:10a, 11)

> **NOTE TO THE TEACHER**
> Every time you teach, you should conscientiously check your own heart. Are you, dear teacher, living what you are teaching? Ask yourself right now, "Am I truly obeying Christ Jesus, the Lord of my life? Your students have observed you. If you are a good example of an obedient Christian, they, too, will want to yield their wills to the will of the Lord Jesus Christ.

THE LESSON

What is your name? (Let each one in your class say his name at the same time.) Names are important. Just suppose that none of us had a name. If I wanted to call one of you up here, I could say, "Will the boy with the striped shirt please come here?" But suppose three of you were wearing striped shirts? Or, what if all of you were dressed alike? We would have a hard time. It is a good thing that each of us has a name.

Some names are very important. Can you tell us the names of some important people in our country? (Wait for answers.)

1. JESUS WANTS US TO GIVE OURSELVES TO HIM
Romans 12:1

The Bible tells us that there is one name which is above every name. (Read Philippians 2:9-10 from your Bible.) What is the name of this Person? Yes, Jesus Christ is His name. And because He is higher than any other person, He is called the *Lord* Jesus Christ.

What does the name "Lord" mean? It is a name for God –Jehovah. Because the Lord Jesus Christ is God the Son, He is Master or Ruler. An earthly master (or lord) is one to whom a person really belongs. The master has power and authority over that person. Perhaps you can think of such a powerful person.

Each country has a president or a king or queen or a dictator who rules the people. Each tribe has a chief who is the ruler. In school, the teacher rules over the pupils. In the home, the parents rule over their children. Rulers are important. Your parents are important. Your teachers are important. The leader of this land is important. But the Lord Jesus Christ is the most important ruler of all. He is greater, wiser, and higher by far than anyone else.

Jesus Christ is so kind and so loving and so great that each one should want to have Him as Lord. But, unfortunately, many people (even those who have been born again through faith in Christ!) do not want Him to be the Lord and ruler of their lives. They want to rule their own lives.

It is marvelous to have Jesus Christ as your Saviour. It is wonderful to know that He has forgiven your sins and that some day He will take you to Heaven. But Jesus wants to be the Lord of your life. He wants you to listen to His Word and obey Him. As a Christian you belong to Him. Perhaps you think that, since Jesus Christ is so great and powerful, He will force you to obey Him. He could, but He does not. He wants you to love and obey Him willingly.

Many hundreds of years ago, it was the custom of the people of God (the Israelites) to have slaves. A man would go to the marketplace where He could buy a slave or servant to work for him. According to the laws, a slaveholder was to be kind to his slaves. The law also said that after the servant had worked for his master six years, the master was to let him go free.

Sometimes, however, after the six years were ended, because he loved his master dearly, the slave did not want to go free. He would say, "I love my master and I will not go out free."

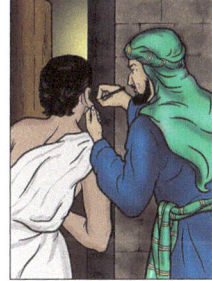

Show Illustration #13

Whenever this happened, the master would bring his slave to the judges of the people. The slave would then stand against the door and let his master bore a hole in his ear with a sharp tool. This hole in his ear would let people know exactly what had happened. From that time on, everyone would know that the servant had chosen to serve his master forever. (See Exodus 21:1-6; Deuteronomy 15:12-17.)

The experience of the slave reminds us that the Lord Jesus Christ paid a great price to buy each one of us out of the slavemarket of sin. We are all born slaves of sin and Satan. The punishment for sin is death. But Jesus wanted us for Himself. He wanted to set us free. The price Jesus paid to save us from sin and death was not paid with money but with His own life. He died in our place. He took the punishment we deserved. He paid this great price so that some day we could live with Him in His eternal home.

Because He has bought us for Himself, He wants us to serve Him. He wants to be our Master, Ruler, and Lord. Think of it–the One who is higher than any king or president on earth wants you. He wants me! He wants us for Himself. He wants to share all His good things with us. But we must first acknowledge Him as Lord of our lives if we want to enjoy fully all His good things. You can choose today to recognize Him as your Lord.

Let us think of some of the reasons why we should have Him as Lord of our lives. (You may remember that we have mentioned some of these things in former lessons.)

2. JESUS IS THE ETERNAL SON OF GOD, CREATOR OF ALL
Hebrews 1:1-2

Show Illustration #14

1. *Jesus is God, the Son.* (See Hebrews 1:1, 2, 8.)

Show Illustration #14A

He is Eternal, with no beginning and no ending, just like God the Father. (See Hebrews 1:8; Micah 5:2.) (The circle in the picture has no beginning and no ending.)

Show Illustration #14B

He is the Creator (along with God the Father) of the universe: Heaven, earth, stars, sun, moon, planets. (See Hebrews 1:2, 10.) He called all things into existence and made everything out of nothing. The Lord Jesus Christ holds everything in place. He keeps the sun shining. He sends the wind and rain and snow. (See Hebrews 1:3 and 1 Corinthians 8:6.)

2. *The Lord Jesus is perfect.* (See 2 Corinthians 5:21.) When Jesus lived on earth He was tested, but He did not sin. Because He was tested, He understands when we are tested and can help us turn away from temptation. (See Hebrews 2:18 and 1 Corinthians 10:13.)

3. JESUS PROVED HE IS LORD BY THE MIRACLES HE DID
Hebrews 2:4

Show Illustration #15

3. *Christ Jesus proved He is the Lord by* the many miracles, signs, and wonders He did while He was on earth. (See Hebrews 2:4.)

Show Illustration #15A

He proved that He is Lord who is able to supply every need. He fed more than 5,000 people with five buns and two fish. Jesus is well able to meet the needs of the hungry, the thirsty, the sick, the sorrowful, and the dying.

Show Illustration #15B

He proved that He is Lord over the elements of nature. He walked on the water and stilled the storm.

Show Illustration #15C

He proved He is the Lord of glory. The brightness within Him shone out before three of His disciples when He talked with Moses and Elijah on the mountain. It was a preview of His future glory.

The miracles that the Lord Jesus did while He was here on earth were not magic tricks. They were acts of real power. Since He is Creator with God the Father, He knows all the secrets of nature. With His almighty power He can do everything. (See John 1:1-3.) His miracles and wonders met human needs in a superhuman way. He overruled the usual forces of nature and showed His power and holiness. What a wonderful Lord!

4. JESUS PROVED HIS POWER OVER SIN AND DEATH
Hebrews 1:3

Show Illustration #16

4. *Jesus Christ proved that He has power over death and over sin.* (See Hebrews 1:3; 1 Corinthians 15:20-28.) He proved it by dying on the cross and rising from the dead after three days. And He is alive forevermore. (See Revelation 1:18.) He is Lord over death. Because of this wonderful fact:

Show Illustration #16A

a) Salvation is offered to all who call upon the name of the Lord. (See Acts 2:21; Romans 10:13.) When He died on the cross He took our sin upon Himself. (See Isaiah 53:6; 1 Peter 2:24.) He paid our death penalty. (See Romans 6:23.)

Show Illustration #16B

b) Jesus has the power to deliver from death (John 5:24)–and from the fear of death (Hebrews 2:15). Because the Lord Jesus Christ rose from the dead, every one of His born again children will rise again.

Show Illustration #16C

c) A day is coming when the Lord Jesus Christ will reign and be King of kings and Lord of lords. (See 1 Timothy 6:15; Revelation 17:14; 19:16.)

The crown in the illustration reminds us of this.) Jesus Christ really is Lord. *God* tells us so. The *Word of God* tells us that He is the Lord. The *disciples* of Jesus called Him Lord. Yet there are many people on earth who will not acknowledge Him as Lord.

The day is coming, however, when everyone in Heaven, in earth and under the earth will bow before Jesus and confess with their tongues that He is Lord. (See Philippians 2:10, 11.) This does not mean that everyone on earth will be saved. You can have everlasting life only if you call upon Him to be your Saviour while you are living here on earth. After death it will be too late. You will know then that He really is the Lord of glory, but you will not be able then to receive Him as your Saviour.

Will you let Him be your Saviour today? Do you believe He is the Son of God? Do you believe He died for your sin? Will you receive Him as your Saviour?

If you have done this, you will love Him so much that you will want to let Him rule your life. He is Jesus (Saviour), Christ, the Lord!

www.ingramcontent.com/pod-product-compliance
Lightning Source LLC
Chambersburg PA
CBHW060806090426
42736CB00002B/172